LOUISIANA SON

Published by Spines
ISBN: 979-8-89569-062-8

LOUISIANA SON

A YOUNG BLACK MAN'S JOURNEY TO IDENTITY

LEO GREGOIRE

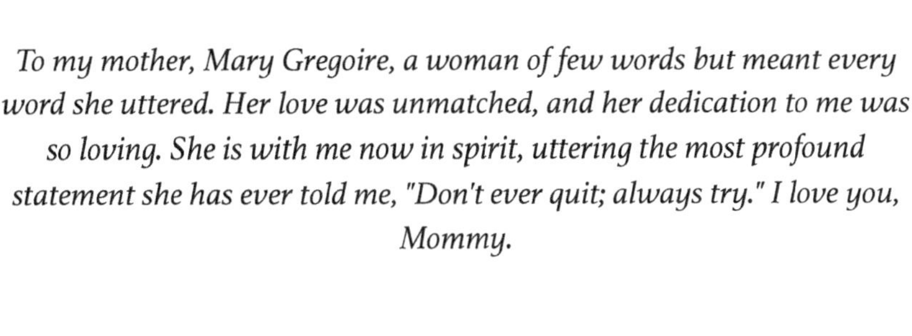

To my mother, Mary Gregoire, a woman of few words but meant every word she uttered. Her love was unmatched, and her dedication to me was so loving. She is with me now in spirit, uttering the most profound statement she has ever told me, "Don't ever quit; always try." I love you, Mommy.

CONTENTS

ACKNOWLEDGMENTS

First and foremost, I would like to express my infinite love and gratitude to the Universe for guiding me on my path of ones and enlightenment. I have sincere love and appreciation for having such a loving and caring family. I want to thank my loving mother, Mary Gregoire (RIP). She is the epitome of what a mother should be raising a boy by herself. She gave me enough rope to hang myself as I learned the many lessons of life growing up as a young boy. Her most famous words to me as I cried to her on the phone when I was stationed in Germany, being denied the privilege of becoming an Army Drill Sergeant. She told me never to quit and always try. Those words have been with me all my life, and I thank her. I want to thank my father, Leo Gregoire Sr. (RIP), as he navigated his life trying to understand who he was and how to be a father to all his kids. I say this with infinite love and gratitude. Thank you for all the fishing trips and for being my weather guide and LSU football friend. To my oldest sister, Charene Gregoire, thank you. You are my everything, and I love you. You are the example of a Big Sister and Big Brother I longed for. You are the epitome of what hustle stands for. You were my driving force behind the 27 years I spent in the United States Army. I saw your rise, fall, and rise again.

You're the Be, Know, and Do to all young entrepreneurs, including myself. I want to thank my sister, Leona Gregoire (RIP) thank you for being my protector, my dance coach, and my best friend. We would argue like cat and dog, and 5 minutes later, it never happened. Thank you for protecting me and teaching me to live my life to the fullest. To my youngest sister, Denita Gregoire, thank you for putting up with your big brother. I know I got on your nerves many days, but I love you wholeheartedly. You made being a Big Brother an honor and a privilege, and I love you so much. To my Brother Micheal Spencer from another mother. Thank you for being an example for me to follow. Many days, I studied you, and you never knew it. From your dress attire, your swag, and how you lived life taking care of your family. Thank you for being an example I emulate and follow. To my youngest sister, Leandra, I love you with all my heart. It is an honor to have met you and to have allowed me to be a part of your life. Your hunger and drive for education inspired me to pursue my education. Thank you, lil sis, and I love you. Thank you to the United States Army and the many brothers and sisters I have had the honor and privilege of serving with. To my ex-wives, Tamara Gregoire and Treshina Durst, thank you for all your mentorship and guidance. You have taught me much and guided me while learning to become a man. Thank you both, and I love you both. Thank you to my best friend in Life, Louis Alexandre; you are my brother and have always looked out for me. Thank you for your loving wisdom and guidance; without you in this book, it would not be a book.

Finally, thank you to my daughter Briana Gregoire; you have made being a father a loving journey. I pray I make you proud of me as I continue my journey. Thank you for giving me three beautiful granddaughters, Addison, Zaniah, and Lalah. I still can spell her name. Thank you for being in my life and being a part of my journey. If it were not for you, I would not have written this book.

Serenity Prayer
Universe, grant me the Serenity to accept the things I cannot change, the courage to change the things I can, and the Wisdom to know the difference.

INTRODUCTION

Being born and growing up can be blessings. For me, I faced many challenges. As a young boy, I was always very sick. As far as I remember, every holiday, I fell gravely ill. My mother would wrap me up in a blanket after rubbing me down with alcohol and sitting by the bed, praying for me to get well. But little did she know God had big plans for me. The neighborhood boys always challenged me because of my small size. As a little boy, I had many dreams and fantasies. I would sit by my window and daydream all day long of flying. As I sat in my window on many mornings looking at Mr. Willy Brown's fig tree, I would investigate the sun and picture myself flying all around the world. As I got older, most things changed: my voice, size, and family dynamics. As an adolescent male, I had a difficult time navigating this world. But I met every challenge with a smile and the grace of majestic Kings.

I loved my adolescent years, eating at all my friends' homes only to be asked when I got home, son, did you eat? Yes, ma'am was my reply. My mother knew then that her son was a survivor, and she kind of let me be me. I just made sure I followed her rules. I did not like school but loved the girls in the school, which I will discuss in more detail in the following chapters. I goofed around so much in school that I graduated 469th out of a class of 500 students. I cannot believe it; I now hold three different degrees. My young adult years were met with the visions of traveling, but this time under the guise of the military, specifically the Army. I gave the Army 27 faithful years, during which I had the pleasure of mentoring, coaching and teaching thousands of Soldiers, but most of all, I traveled the world and made my dream come true. As I write this book, I am so grateful for the position I am in now. Having lived a full life of parties, hard work and coming out of my comfort zone, I have learned that living this life is so beautiful and full of adventure, from the little boy who would sit in his room looking over Mr. Willy Brown's fig tree gazing into the sun wanting to fly, to a beautiful soul looking to spread infinite love and gratitude wherever he goes. Always remember these words, never quit, and always try. Thank you, Mommy, and now thank you. Please enjoy reading about lil Leo.

FEBRUARY 21ST, 1968

At 3:18 AM, Leo John Gregoire Jr or II I am still a little confused was born 7 lbs. 8 ounces. I was a very healthy baby boy. To this day, I am so very grateful for that day. But boy, the days to come had adventure, pain, misery and love attached to my DNA. You see, being the only boy in the family, you had no one in the house to play with. But when my youngest sister showed up on October 18th, 1970, now someone to play with. What was great about being the only boy in the family you would think I was spoiled and got anything and everything I wanted. Heck, growing up with three sisters and me being the only boy, you would think this is possible. Heck no, it was the complete opposite, lol. My mother was hard but fair and was the greatest and wisest mentor and kid I could have. My dad was a special man and a special case. He was a very hard-working man. My dad worked for Kingston Construction Company, and from what I was told, he could operate every machine in the construction industry at that time. As a young boy, I remember waiting many days for my father to get off work and eat the sandwiches he did not eat and get a little taste of the beer he did not want. I will tell you the rest as we progress in the book. My father was a man who had to find himself. Many times, as I grew older, I was told he was the bell of the ball, sort to say. How is it that a boy could have a mother who was stronger than life itself but as quiet as could be and did not like the limelight? But my father, you best believe he made an entrance anywhere he went. Yes, he was the man teaser and the women pleaser. This is why he was not around a lot during the many times I fell gravely ill. I love my father, and he had to walk his path in life and rest in peace. He did that no matter the cost. My mother, on the other hand, was the epitome of what a single mother was. She single-handedly raised four kids, three girls and one boy. So why am I talking so much about my parents versus me? You see, I was a combination of both. As a young boy, I was very shy, but I loved the attention I received. But let me digress. I am getting way ahead of myself.

WHEN IT ALL BEGAN

As a baby, there were not many stories told of me and told to me. But I had baby pictures to show how happy I was a healthy baby at first; then, I started to become sick as I got a little older. I remember being sick many times, and it seemed like me and the month of December did not get along. As soon as December 1st hit, I would start getting sick, not just once but all the time. It seemed like when I hit the age of 2 years old, I was getting sick every holiday season. I remember getting sick from Thanksgiving through Christmas and New Year's. I would get very sick, and my mother would do her best with all the home remedies, which I practice today. Castor oil with aspirin and coke was the number one killer of all sickness in our home.

A mixture of honey and baking soda followed me. I haven't tried that one yet. But I remember always throwing up and not wanting to eat. My mother always knew when her son did not want to eat, he was sick. I guess I was a human garbage disposal. But there was one time I will never forget. I became so ill that my mother tried to reach my father, but he was asleep at another lady's home, which I will discuss in later chapters. My mother was afraid and felt I needed to go to the emergency room. My mother called the lady's home. My mother asked to speak with my father, and she told my mother that my father was asleep and she did not want to wake him. I remember my mother rubbing my body down with alcohol and wrapping me up in a blanket. She sat at the end of my bed, praying over me all night long. This part is very emotional because I remembered it like it was yesterday. By the next morning, my fever had broken, and I was feeling a lot better. This would happen every holiday season. Not that I did not love the holidays, especially Christmas, but I would get sick from the day after Thanksgiving all the way to Christmas. Even now, as I write this book, I can still remember always getting better for when it was time to open the Christmas presents, which are coming in the future chapters.

MY DREAMS AND IMAGINATION

At a very young age, I grew the most vivid imagination possible. I remember always sitting in my back room, looking out of my window, looking at Mr. Willy Brown's fig tree, imagining that I could fly. The sun would look so beautiful to me that I would sit there for hours. Now, at a young age, and I do mean a young age, I had crushes on many girls. Yes, I am getting to my dreams. I remember in the first grade, I had a crush on her, and she was the most beautiful girl in the world. I would imagine just sitting by her would make me the happiest kid in the world. But the crushes got even better when I had a crush on our next neighbor's oldest daughter, nicknamed Nessa. Nessa was the most beautiful girl I had ever seen. And let me tell you, I could not wait to go to sleep so I could dream about her. Now let me tell you, if I knew I had lucid dreams, then, like wow, I had them. I would dream I was jumping out of our back bathroom window and hopping the fence to look for Nessa. Sometimes I found her, and sometimes I did not, but when I found her, I gave her a very big kiss—not knowing that this would lead to a life of kissing many women, lol. But most of my dreams were beautiful, and the skies were beautiful in my dreams. If Nessa only knew she was my childhood crush as a kid, she would laugh and giggle. Now, like I said, I have many vivid and lucid dreams. But there were those dreams that I rarely talk about, even to this day. It was only recently that I could talk about these dreams or nightmares. I had one dream as a child, in which at the end of my bed, there was an image with red eyes and horns. It was the scariest image I had seen in my life. This dream would traumatize me even up to this day. This dream became the catalyst for my becoming scared of the dark. In another dream, a horned-like figure grabbed me by my legs and drugged me through our house. Even at this age, I remember this dream. But the scariest dream I ever had; I still cannot describe it to this day. It looks like a dark figure from a distance with fireworks coming from it. Sometimes, I think it's from one of my past lives when a world was being destroyed. I will save this story for the end. But again, my dreams, even to this day, have been prophetic, with many premonitions and lucid. Again, this story will be the last chapter of this book.

CHRISTMAS LIGHTS

As a child, if there is one thing I remember more than anything else, it is Christmas. I was so mesmerized by the Christmas lights. Lawd, you would think that if those lights were books in a classroom, I would be a genius. No matter how sick I was as a kid, I always got better by Christmas day. I remember waking up in the middle of the night and sneaking into the kitchen just so I could look at our Christmas lights. Heck, I am the same way today, still mesmerized by Christmas lights. I remember always trying to sneak a peek at what was in the presents for me. I remember one year I saved up all my allowance, which was a nickel, then it graduated to a quarter and buying my mother some deodorant and my daddy some shaving cream. When I think of it makes me giggle a little, but it was from my heart, and I think they loved it.

Every Christmas, we would go to bed early for some reason or another. My older sisters would go to midnight mass because we were catholic, and after it was over, they would go and hang out with me at our cousin's house. To me, this was the Super Bowl of Christmas to be able to go to midnight mass and then go to my cousin's home. So overrated. I remember when I was old enough to go and then went to my cousin's house. Man, I could have stayed at home. Christmas was always a good day for us. On Christmas day, we would put on our Christmas clothes, go to church, and then visit all our relatives. Man, it seemed like a marathon with no end in sight. All I wanted to do was eat the cake at everyone's house. With all Christmas celebrations, we had great ones, but then we had some that were sad. This one year, it seems like I got every toy I wanted. I couldn't believe it. I wanted every Tonka truck that was being made, and it seemed like I hit the jackpot when I got one. I remember just being so happy that day. My dad was home, and he was saying Son, do you like the toys I brought you. Now, sometimes my daddy is there with us on Christmas day, and sometimes he is not, but this one day, he was there. I remember him saying Son, do you like the toys I brought you and me saying yes, sir, thank you for all the toys you brought me. But something was strange about this: my oldest sister left the room when he made that statement. So, after a while, he left to do his thing, and my mother called me to talk with me.

Now, my mother was hard but fair, but she had a loving way to talk to you if she knew it was going to hurt you. I remember this like it was yesterday. She said Leo Jr, your daddy did not buy you any toys this year. Your older sister did. It felt like I was hit in the chest with a sledgehammer. It broke my heart, and all I could do was go outside and play. My mother's loving voice still resonates as I can still hear her say these words. To this day, I have forgiven my father, but the love I have for my mother and how she broke the news to me was the love of an angel.

ELIZABETH STREET

Growing up in New Iberia, Louisiana, living on Elizabeth Street was such a joy and a treat. My neighborhood was the greatest growing up as a kid. We had more fun than bad. Most of the friends I played with were the best. Maybe one of them would be a pic of me that, from time to time, made me cry, but overall, it was a joy. I remember how we would play hide and seek when we were allowed to play after the dark primary when it was not a school night. It was my two friends and me, and we were a team. I can remember we would crawl under the house to get some soft dirt. Now, our house is set up on some 18-inch bricks, so if it got flooded, the water would not come into the house. But we would crawl under the house and sift through the dirt to get some soft dirt. We played many games, baseball, in one of the fields next to my house. The older kids seem like they could hit that ball into space.

We played a game called 3 Steps, which is more like a triple-long jump. I will not lie; I think we could have been Olympians if we had stuck to it. Many of our parents would always sit outside and talk to each other. There was one rule: do not leave the street. Heavens, if you left off the street, you got the whipping of a lifetime.

I can remember my mother telling me to put my shoes on and stop running in the yard and the street barefoot. But what my mother did not understand was that when you took the shoes off and ran, you could run faster. So many times, I broke this rule. I remember I got a nail in my foot, and my mother told me I was going to whip you first, then doctor on you. Yes, she did it in that order. When it came to the holidays, and I was not sick, we had this thing called firecracker wars. Now, this was the next level. We would go and battle other neighborhoods when it come to this. Or we would battle the people down the street. The aim was to hit your opponent with a rocket. If you had a long PCV valve that was 12 feet in length, this was considered canon. Many times, this battle would go on for hours until the winner was declared. We had many different types of people living on our street. I was such a skinny kid that the older kids would give me a hard time when it came to joining in and playing with them, but eventually, they would let me play. As a small kid, I was bullied many times, but it was not so severe that the ones bullying me did not love me and take care of me once I left the neighborhood. We had one girl, and I mean this one girl. Carol was stocking built, and everyone feared her. I saw her wrestle one of the older kids in our neighborhood, which was bigger than her. She pinned him down on the ground and would not let him up. All I remember is she pushed his head on the concrete and made him cry. As time went on, she and my second oldest sister, Leona, were supposed to fight. I was like, man, she is going to beat my sister up. But now, well and behold, they never fought and have become the best of friends. My neighborhood was the greatest, and it will always be known as Elizabeth Street.

MY FAMILY

Growing up in our household as the only boy had some advantages but not very many. I will say that as I got older, I got my own room, which is the only perk I had as the only boy in the family. Now, my sisters Charlene, Leona and Denita are the best sisters a boy could ever have because they all filled a special part of my life. Charlene was the oldest, and let me tell you, she was the example to follow. She is seen a lot in our household, and to this day, she is an example of hustle and determination. She taught me how to play chess, checkers, and basketball, you name it. My oldest sister taught me a lot. She was very smart and hard-working. I remember her working at McDonalds and bringing home sometimes some burgers for us to eat. My second to oldest sister, Leona, was the treat of all my sisters. We were born four years apart, 2 hours apart on the same day. How did they have good timing? Well, I cannot go into that, lol. Then there is my heart, my little Sister Denita, with whom she and I spent most of our time. As her big brother, I was her protection and best friend. That's until our adult years when I learned how to get back on her nerves like she would me. My mother was the epitome of hard work. My mother, Mary Gregoire, was hard but fair. She would make sure we had a game night where we would play many games like Scrabble, monopoly, bingo, you name it. If there was a game out there, we played it. Then, there was my father, Leo Gregoire, who was a hardworking man. As I was growing up, I now know my father had to find himself, so our home life with him was rough. He and my mother would fuss and fight a lot. I remember one night I was awakened by my mother and father fighting, but low, well and behold, on each side of my mother was my two older sisters helping my mother fight my daddy. What a sight that I can still see to this day. The only thing I could do at that time was shout stop it. Not that they heard me. My father taught me how to fish and cut the grass, but let me not cut that grass on time. It was a whole different story. My mother was the chief disciplinarian in the household, which means she gave me all the whippings. My dad would just pop me in the head if I did something wrong. But I remember him whipping me once in my whole life because he never had to; I was afraid of my dad back then. I loved all the members of my family. We loved each other, and we made the best of times when we needed it.

CORPUS CHRISTI TEXAS

I remember, as a young boy, the move we made to Corpus Christi. I did not know that the move was for us to leave my father behind. I did not know until some years later that my mother was secretly packing us up little by little for us to make the move. I remember getting on that Grey Hound bus leaving New Iberia, Louisiana and arriving in Houston, Texas. From what I remember, all our belongings were in some suite cases and some in trash bags. Being this young, you really don't know what is going on. My only thought was when we would be headed back. Living with my aunt was okay; for the most part, she enjoyed having us there. I remember being in a location that was foreign to me. A kid from the country is now in the city. A kid from a predominantly black town to now a predominantly Hispanic city. During this time, my aunt had four boys. I will leave their names out of the book, but the two youngest boys still lived with their mother, and their ages were 16 and 14 years old. The older 2 were the ones I fell in love with, and I will tell you more as I go further into the story. We didn't have much, and I did not mind wearing second-hand and even third-hand clothes. Heck, they were brand new clothes to me, and I love them. As I got integrated into the neighborhood, I started making new friends. Some were nice, and some were mean. But overall, we all got along. I spent a lot of time alone, and my youngest cousin would let me ride his bike. But everything went south when I accidentally flattened his tire. He became the worst of the worst. All I can say is the bullying went to a different level with the youngest two boys. My oldest sister was with us for a few years, and then she left and went to college. My second oldest sister, Leona, fit in like a glove. Heck, she learned how to cuss in Spanish, lol. This girl didn't miss a beat. We lived right next to a park so I would be in the park most of the time. But when the park was crowded with kids, this is when my youngest cousin would have at me. He would tell everyone in the neighborhood that I would urinate on myself and that we were poor and I was wearing the clothes he gave me. Now, this was not the 2nd to youngest but the youngest. He was more verbally abusive. This went on the whole summer, and let me tell you, it was rough for Leo. I know this is why I do not like bullies to this day, and I need to heal this wound. My aunt was married. I will call him uncle. He did not say much to me, and I never heard him say much to anyone. Now during this time, I was going to an elementary school named Minger Elementary. This is when my liking for girls picked up a lot. And man, let me tell you, I was like a kid in a candy store. I thought every girl was beautiful. I remember this one kid named Abel, but he and I did not get along. And one day in the park, it came to a head, and we got into a fight. Now let me go back; I did not do well with fights. I remember my first fight in New Iberia; I went to a free lunch in the park one summer, and I got into a fight. And let me tell you, if my tongue were the weapon of choice, I would have won that fight, but my hands could not keep up with my mouth, and I lost that fight and hit the streets running, lol. Well, back to the story, so Abel and I got into a fight, and let me tell you something happened: my hands were faster than my mouth, and I won that fight. Now, I was on top of the world until Mary Gregoire showed up my mother. She did not want her kids fighting, especially me. This is one of the reasons why I would get beat up so much because she structs the fear of God in me. If you fight, you will go to jail. And she meant it. So, when she saw me acting up in the park, my mother gave me the whipping of a lifetime. It seemed like I was getting whippings every day. But before that, my second-to-oldest cousin was at the house. And let me tell you, everyone in the neighborhood was afraid of him. When he came outside, there was a crowd, and kids wanted to get at me because I beat up Abel, but he was a little bigger than me. But cousin dared anyone to touch me, or they would have to deal with him. He was a true gangster in every sense of the word. I did not mention the oldest cousin. He was serving time, to my understanding, and when I saw him for the first time, I was like, lawd, he is a bodybuilder. He was the best first cousin I could have. I remember one time we went swimming, and again, I thought this came naturally, but it didn't. Those youngest two cousins threw me in the water, and I almost wanted to drown. Yes, it was 3 feet, but it felt like 12 feet. I remember the oldest being a lifeguard, and he put me on his back and swam the length of the pool with me on his back. He was the greatest. Now, my mother was gone most of the time. My aunt would cook, and it seemed like we only ate rice and fried chicken the whole summer long. I was sick and tired of eating white rice with no gravy, and you know, being from Louisiana, we need gravy. And the fried chicken was so bland. Lawd, what is going on here? Now, every Sunday, my mother and aunt would go to the Kingdom Hall because my mother was becoming one of Jehovah's Witnesses. So, when they were gone, I would steal the cakes, the little doughnut-like cakes. I can't remember what they were called, but I would steal some and eat them, and they tasted good. Thinking that the bullying would not happen when both my aunt and mother were gone was a green light for these 2 to have their way with me. They would push me around and beat me up, not brutally but enough to make me cry. I was miserable when my mother and aunt would leave. These guys would put toilet paper in my eyes. These two did not care about anything but making my life miserable. This went on for the whole summer. Then it finally happened. I got tired of them beating me up, and I started fighting back. I was tired of crying and had no choice but to be scared, but I was ready to fight. It was at this time they left me alone, and the bullying was minimal every day from that day. Sometimes, you must be sick and tired to make a change. Well, everything came to a head when my mother and my uncle got into an argument. My aunt did not know what to do. But if you know Mary Gregoire like I know her, she was not going to back down. Hell, she just left a combat zone dealing with Leo Gregoire Sr, so you know she is a combat veteran and war-tested. Little did I know she had found us an apartment and was going to move us. Well, that move happened sooner than later. She packed us up, put everything in trash bags, and we went out. Lawd, I was never happier. Let's go. I did not care where we went; I wanted out of that house. I was tired of eating rice, no gravy and bland fried chicken.

TRADEWINDS APARTMENTS

When we showed up at Tradewinds Apartments, we did not have much. Heck, I think we only had the clothes and what we were wearing in our trash bags. Some will say the best time of your life is when you do have a lot. Now, for me, I had to figure out how to use public transportation, so it was big boy time. My little sister and I would catch the city bus to our school because it was not summer, and we still had two months left before school ended. I will never forget that we would have to catch the bus to the rough side of town and then to the elementary school we went to, Menger Elementary. If we were lucky, we could catch the connecting bus, which was the Leopard and Calallen bus. Most of the time, we were not that fortunate. We would have to wait almost 2 hours for the bus to come. At this time, I was 11 years old, so Mary Gregoire knew I could take care of my little sister and get us home. I remember meeting my best Mel. He was my best friend at that time. We would sometimes go and play in the woods all day long. We did not even think there could be a rattlesnake, but we did not care. We were having fun. Now, I mentioned we did not have much. As an explorer who always wanted to make my mother happy, I would see furniture in the dumpster that no one wanted. I would hop in and grab it. Take it home and say, Mommy, I got us this. And we used it. There was a time I found a couch and could not carry it myself. Guess who helped me carry it?

Mary Gregoire, my mother. Now, some of the furniture needed cleaning. One time I remember the furniture having chiggers in them, so it did not last long. I had many friends living in this apartment complex. We would play sports, you name it. I got myself a side job working as a maintenance boy for the apartment complex. The manager was ok, but she later got me in trouble, and I got the worst whipping and last whipping of my life. My mother gave me free rein to run the streets of Corpus Christi as long as I was in the dark. I would go fishing—sometimes Mel and I would go by myself.

I remember carrying my fishing pole and bucket on the bus and loving life. See, I had to catch the city bus to get to the T Head to go fishing about 10 miles away. Yes, my mother trusted her 11-year-old son to be home before dark. Now, my mother works as a hotel maid. I remember we would go and help, and this was my introduction to fixing my bed the correct way, which helped me later in life when I joined the Army. My little sister and I would go and help her out. She would give us some change to go to McDonald's right across the street.

Man, life was good. We could go swimming but could not swim. So, guess what? My little sister and I started teaching each other how to swim. I think if we had remained in Corpus Christi, we would be Olympic swimmers; that's how determined we were to learn how to swim. Now, as time went on and the summer was coming to a close, I had a summer job. I remember working for the apartment complex manager. I had odd jobs like cleaning up apartments that people left dirty, but most of my money was made when she and I would clean up the Century 21 buildings at night. That's where most of my money went to. I remember one of my checks being 72 dollars, and now, to me, that was millionaire status. However, this job was short-lived when the apartment manager and I had different opinions. Yes, I, at that age, would have a different opinion. I really came to a head when one of the apartment windows got busted, and I guessed who was to blame. Yes, it was me. Because I was a kid who was always in the neighborhood playing, I was the fault guy. When the news hit my mother, I was wrong in more ways than you can shake a stick at. Now, this event still sits with me because this was the worst and last whipping I had ever received. My mother whipped me so badly and for so long that I still remember it. And the whole time, I told her I did not do it. She did not listen to me. And I kept whipping me. Before she died some years prior to that, I finally forgave her for whipping me. I have always loved my mother, but for the first time in my life, I was not guilty of the infraction.

DRISCOLL JUNIOR HIGH SCHOOL

Now, when I tell you that I did not get along with my aunt's youngest sons, I did not. But they were the ones who told me about Driscoll Junior High. They told me they were stabbings and fighting 24 hours of the day. And I was scared out of my pants to go to this school. But I had no choice, so I headed to Driscoll. My cousin, for the first time in my life, was not telling me a lie. This school was rough. Gangs in the school fight almost every other day, no less than once a week. Now, the good part about going to Driscoll was there were a lot of good-looking girls, and at my age, that was the focus. Of course, I was too small to play sports, and I was in the 7th grade. I remember being kicked by the one student who had transferred there, and I did not retaliate because he would have beat me up. Yes, he was a gang member, and Leo did not want any part of that. Driscoll sat between the Hispanic side of town and the black side of town. It was not good for Leo because I had no friends until I met this one kid. I will call him Z. He was a big guy, and I don't know how it came to be that he and I would become friends. I remember getting slapped behind my head and coming out of the bathroom crying, and Z found the guy who did it and almost beat him up. I thank God for Z because he protected me. I met another guy I will call T. Now, he and I were the same size, so man, it felt good to have someone I could relate to. You know, I had no fighting skills, and my strength game was not up to par. I remember this one class. Now I am in the seventh grade and the one black girl I will call her L. She put me in the headlock, and I swear I think she was trying to kill me. Man, I had never been put in a headlock like this before. Needless to say, my seventh-grade year came and went with quickness, and let me tell you, the 8th grade is where all the magic started to happen.

8TH GRADE

My 8th grade year was truly magical. Now, the school has not changed much, and the fights have increased, but that was not an issue for me. I now knew how to navigate around the school, and that's all that mattered. I remembered one of my teachers, Mrs. Harris, and all the black guys had a crush on her. So, if the tough guys did not pay attention to me, I would have been in the clear. Me and T started hanging out more. I would go to his house from time to time. See, at this time, we had moved from Tradewinds apartments to a house on Manchester Street. I met new friends, and life was good. Now, like I said in the beginning, the 8th grade was magical because now I am all about the girls. Yes, I said it. I am a young boy with hormone problems. I remember meeting more new friends, and I was loving life. I remember that in this one class, there was one girl who completely ignored my many jokes. And one day, she and I got into an argument, and yours truly won the argument. She sat in front of me. I will call her my crush. But out of the blue, one day, my jokes penetrated her and she was dying laughing at my many jokes. Like I said, my 8th grade year was magical. What was crazy was that the 9th-grade star running back hung out with me and T. He was a big guy, but for some odd reason, we were a trio. My mother, who was working a lot, finally gave in and let me play school sports, so the first sport for school was Basketball. Now, I was not as good as I thought I was, but we had this one guy. I am going to call him M. This guy was the next Micheal Jordan on our team. He would make a shot from anywhere on the court. No team and no one could stop him, and we won all our games. I did not play much, but heck, we won. Now, currently, everyone in the class and probably knows me and my crush like each other a whole lot. We were always talking and laughing. One day, I went home, and I was hit with the news: we were heading back to New Iberia for a few days. Now, to me, I am like, heck yeah, let's go. So, we went home for a few days, maybe a week, then we returned to Corpus Christi. Now, a lot has changed since we were in New Iberia. My mother told me it was okay for me to run track, which I did, but now my crush has a boyfriend and a man, and I did not like that. When I found out, I had not talked to her for as long as I could remember. I will call him R. He and I played on the same basketball team, and he was a pretty boy. Man, he was cute, lol. But she would try to talk to me, and I would not say words to her. So, I went and got a girlfriend. Now this girl was stranger than me, and I thought I was strange. But we made it work. So, there is a school announcement. There is a school dance. Now let me tell you I was not a dancer and did not know any moves. Later in life, that would change. But I remember showing up to the dance and dancing with my new girlfriend. She was like you cannot dance, and people were looking at me like this guy is stiffer than 2x4. So now I am embarrassed, and something happened to where I left her alone at the dance, and she went dancing with another guy. I did not care. My heart was with my crush, who was there with her now boyfriend R. But somehow, through all the crowd and the music, she came up to me and, grabbed my hand and brought me onto the dance floor. She was the best dancer in the building, and she was the prettiest girl at the dance. I remembered it like yesterday. The song Call Me by Midnight star was playing. She was looking me in the eyes, and all I could do was smile. This was a beautiful night for me. So, as the days go by, I am on the track team and going to class messing with all the girls being Mr. Flirtatious. I was friends with a lot of girls, and a lot of girls liked me. Yes, this guy's hormones were elevated. One day, I went home, and Mary Gregoire asked each of her children do you want to move back to New Iberia and I said heck yeah. Not realizing we would never come back or move back to Corpus again. Now, this was heartbreaking because now I don't want to leave school. The word is out, and my crush and I like each other a lot. She and her boyfriend broke up. Now everyone is like, when is Leo and his crush going to get together? But I had to break the news I was moving back to Louisiana. Man, I did not want to leave. I had made new friends and had a loving life. I will never forget the last day I was a student at Driscoll. It was a sad day. I remember my crush and I just trying every way to see each other throughout the day. I will never forget when the bell rang for me to go to my bus. Some of my classmates brought my crush to me. My crush and I went to a quiet part of the school. She was crying, and I was sad. This day I will never forget. We held hands, and we hugged. then it finally happened: she gave me the softest, loveliest, most sensual kiss I had ever received in my life. As I write this, I can still feel this kiss because this was my first kiss, a tongue-and-lips kiss. It was almost like an angel kissing me. I was in love with my crush from that time on. As I got on the bus, I wished everything would change, not knowing that I would never see my crush again. Truly my first kiss and my first crush. Later in life, I would see her again, and we would laugh about that day. I will never forget my 8th-grade year.

BACK IN NEW IBERIA

Moving back to New Iberia was very different. We did not live in the old house from which we had moved. Later in life, my mother told me that my daddy was given the choice of keeping the house or driving his car. Well, he kept the car. I cannot say anything negative about that because my priorities are just now coming online. But we lived with my daddy, who was renting out one of our cousin's rented homes. It was clear my father was not there much and did not want to have much to do with us.

On the other hand, I had to go to Anderson Street Junior High and meet new friends. This was not too hard because I had cousins and friends in the school. But everyone had grown up now, like 13 and 14 years of age. So now I am in school, and man, everyone is big. I had grown a little, but these guys had beards and were alums of the school. This tells you how long some of these guys were in the school. Now, one day, I am in school, and word is out there of a cute guy, and all the girls are getting ready to meet this guy. I am like, who is this guy? Little did I know it was me. Now you know, when I found out years later that I was the cute guy in the school, I probably would have opened myself up even more. Now, I could not play sports for the school because I had arrived there just as the school year was about to end. Now, being the new guy in the school, I did not know how popular I was. I met this girl who had become my puppy love, and I won't say her name, but let me tell you. We went on a school trip, and she and I kissed the whole way back from the trip.

I was in love. Little did I know that I had not been taught anything about the birds and the bees. One night, and let me tell you, I now know I have premonitions; I had a dream that she was going to break up with me. Like clockwork, she broke up with me because she said I was too jealous-hearted. This broke my heart. I wanted to end my life. It hurt me so badly. I did not get over that hurt for the next two years. But let me tell you when I say that puppy love hurts just as much as grown people love it really do. But I have learned a valuable lesson now as I am older. My summer months were spent hanging out with my new friends and relatives and working for all my relatives, cutting their yards and making me some spare change.

Now, during this time, dancing, popping, and break dancing were the only things. More so popping, and let me tell you, I was so intrigued with learning how to pop it was unreal. In my beginning days, I was stiffer than cardboard. My cousins would laugh at me, trying to pop on the block where we hung out. Little did they know I was so determined to learn that I would spend hours of my day in my room practicing. The following year, I was battling the best poppers in the neighborhood and the town. Yep, me, so I can tell you that with determination, you can achieve anything you put your mind to.

TROPHIES

So, as I started a new school year, I was given a choice. I could have gone to the 9th grade, but that meant I would have been with those giants of kids from the year prior. You see, my education records did not follow me, so the school did not know what to do with either pushing me up to the 9th grade or me staying in the 8th grade another year. I asked them one question: can I still play football if I stay in the 8th grade? Their reply was yes, and it was game on for me. Yes, I am not given the opportunity to play football for my school. The year prior, I went to the award ceremony and saw one of the star athletes become the most valuable player in all three sports for the school. I thought to myself this would be the achievement of a lifetime for me. So here it goes. I am now on the school football team. I was the tailback, and man; It was fun until I got hurt and had to sit out. So, I lost the position but got a chance to move to receiver. I never forgot we had an ok year, but we were ok. I remember one game where the school bully was my lead block on a kickoff return. Yep, he was tough, and I remember doing a kickoff for 70-plus yards. The girl that broke my heart the year prior was recognizing me again. But we did not get back together for years later, which I will save for later in the story. Once football season was over, I had the chance to play basketball for our school. I was the center, and we again were ok. Now we had one game and let me tell you, I was the star. Now, in every game at school, they would announce who the star player was, and in this one game, I had triple-doubles. Yes, my name and I were announced as such. I am famous now, but we had track season to look forward to, and guess what? Yes, I was on the track team running the 100-yard dash, the 4x100 and the 200. Now I totally sucked at the 200, but I could sprint. Now, our track team was not the greatest, but we had all the fun in the world. Now comes the big day. We are at the end of the school year, and yes, I have no girlfriends, but a lot of girls like me. For some odd reason, I did not give them the time of day. But before school was closed, we had our award ceremony. I was excited because my mother was coming. Now, my mother worked very hard and could not come to any of my games. So, I was excited for her to come. Now, my father showed up for this event, so I was really surprised. I did not have much to say because he never came to games, and there were a few times earlier in my life when he would drop me off at baseball practice and not come and pick me up. So, the award ceremony is in full effect, and it is announced. The recipient of the all-around most valuable player is Leo Gregoire. Finally, I have achieved what I set my mind and heart to do, which was to receive this award. But I am looking at my mother, who had the calmest face ever, and my dad is happier than I am. He was celebrating more than me, and all I could remember was he was not even coming to my games, picking me up from a game or watching me practice. He was claiming his son on his achievement. Before I close out this part of the story, it was later in life that my father would apologize to me, not in his words but in his actions. No matter how much he was not in my life, he was in my life for a reason.

FRESHMAN HIGH SCHOOL

By this time of my life, I was starting to really get into who I was. We had moved from my father's home to this one house, and we were quickly evicted because my mother could not afford the rent. No matter how hard it was on her, she never let us see it. My mother was a Jehovah's Witness and remained faithful during our hard times. We finally found a place to live next to our cousin's house. Now, this was a very special time in our life. We had more fun living in this house because we became closer as a family. This house had no electricity, and we moved in during the wintertime. By this time, my mother did not have to worry about me. When it came to my meals, I ate at my friends' houses. I was a hustler, and I knew how to survive. My mother did not have the money to buy me nice things. Many times, after we had PE at school if the kids left clothes behind, I would scoop them up, clean them, and call them mine. Yes, I was a hustler. But the 9th grade was very special because both the Junior high schools came together at this one school because it was the only 9th-grade school in our town outside of the catholic schools. Man, did we have fun? I played football there and was a tight end, and I remember making a touchdown before being moved permanently to defensive because I could tackle. Again, this school was fun until I started getting into trouble. Yes, I got into a fight with a guy who would later in my life become a man I respect, but I also knew he would hurt me as well as he is, knowing I would hurt him. Well, not now, because I am now on my spiritual journey. One day, at my locker that we once shared, he started bullying me, and we got into it. He could not fight, which made it easy for me to pick him up, throw him down and hit him one time. Easy victory, I thought. In my town, during Mardi Gras season, we would go to the town nearby to celebrate because of the parades. So, after the parade, I managed to get close to home, and he came. Something told me it was not over with him. He called my name. I was like, it's on again. Let me go to work on him. And out of nowhere, he pulled a box cutter out and tried to cut my back open. Now, back then, I had cheetah speed, so I ran home and grabbed some knives to go back and cut him up. Mary Gregoire was like what are you doing, and where are you going with those knives. I ignored her and went back to find him. When I found him, not only was I about to get him, but now he had a 2x4, and he swung it at me. I ran back home to find something big enough to get him. Now let me tell you something about Mary Gregoire. She is a woman of her word, and when she says something, she means it. My mother told me if I took one more thing out of her house, she was going to call the cops on me. Of course, I ignored her and grabbed what I needed because I was in combat mode. I will never forget this day; my mother said Son, sit down. The cops are on the way to pick you up. Now, I did not believe her, and I wanted to call her bluff. Like my name is Leo John Gregoire Jr, the cops are knocking at the door. My heart hit the ground, and I was scared. Now I am going to jail. Once they got the report from me, needless to say, the guy never had any issues again. To this day, we respect each other with love. Now, my 9th grade year was the year my sports career was in full bloom. I was on the basketball team, and we won every game. I was the second-string center. Our football team went undefeated. Now let me go back during the school year; the guys who ran track for Center Street

Junior High always joked about us who went to Anderson Street Junior High. We were rivals all in the same school. But little did they know I spent the whole summer lifting weights, getting my strength game together. I remember that at track practice, the coach put us on the line, and I had to show them who I was. I outran all of them except 2 of them. As the season went on, and I was on the 4x100, 100, and 4x400, the coach wanted us to see who was the fastest. Finally, I received the coveted fastest guy on the track team. Too easy for me. We went undefeated in all our track meets. It was said that our 3rd and anchor leg of the 4x100 was the best handoff in the state. These guys were poetry in motion. Now, I don't know if you all remember, but I was one of the best poppers in my town. I remember making the newspaper because I was in a dance contest. I knew I was sure to win, but I lost to one of my dearest friends. Now, he did not beat me in popping, but he could break dance, dam he got me, and I took second place. Later, we would laugh it off and become the best of friends.

THE WHOLE FAMILY

Summertimes in New Iberia could be adventurous for a young man like me. I was still too young to have a job, but I would do odd jobs for my uncle, grandmother and aunts. So, this is how I earned my money to go to all the parties and dances. So, I was always employed, and there was always a party to go to. I remember always hanging out on the corner with my cousins, and all we did was dance. Since popping was the thing, this is what we did day in and day out. I remember this one time and or event that would shut down my whole summer. I remember coming from one of the dances, and I was hanging out with a girl that I had grown up with. We were like brothers and sisters because we were the same age and went to the same school. I remember this one night: this girl who we all went to school with was out with us. This girl was known for being a troublemaker. I never forget this night. The girl and I got into an argument, and she called my mother the B word. I did not take it too kindly to anyone saying anything about my mother. Once she said, my reflexes kicked in, and I punched her in the nose. I did not realize the damage I had done, but when it happened, the girl I grew up with told me to go home. When I got home, I told my mother what had happened, and in Mary

Gregoire's typical wisdom, she asked me one question: am I the B word? I immediately told my mother no, you are not. Then, just as calm as she could be, she replied that there was no need to hit that girl or anyone that calls me the B word. Well, the next day, I thought nothing about getting a knock on the door. Four guys are standing at the door. They were the girls' cousins. Evidently, I did more damage than I realized; I had broken the girl's nose, and this was her cousins coming to my home to get justice. They asked me why I had hit her and if I realized I had broken her nose. Now I am scared because the one cousin who was questioning was a known guy. If he wanted to, he could have grabbed me out of the house, and all of them could have beat me to a pulp. I apologized for what I had done, but it was too late, and the damage was done. Now I am scared, and the word on the street is if they catch me, they are going to beat me and be me bad. I stayed in the house all day long. I did not even go outside during the daytime. If I went outside, it was under the cover of darkness so that no one could see me. What a way to live. So, we are getting towards the end of the summer, and now we are having back-to-school parties. So, thinking everything was okay, I decided to go to one. Well, this one is across town, and I am by myself. So, the party is lit. We are getting our dance on in this place. Now the word is out, and the girls' cousins are in the place looking for me. They made an oath they would not fight me on one. They wanted to hurt me. I am trapped, and I am now scared. So, out of nowhere, one of my cousins is on the spot. Now, this cousin is known in our town, and his family is well-known. He saw the fear in my eyes and asked me what was going on. I told him that the group of guys wanted to jump me. Now, at this time, one of my next-door neighbors, who I grew up with an old guy, came up, shook our hands and asked what was going on. At this point, I am feeling relieved I have two people who have my back. Lawd is about to be a good day. All I wanted was out of this place and back home. Now, I did not know that my cousin was going to approach every-one, but he did. He told me to come on; we got you. I am like, ok, let's go. He went outside, and the group of guys walked up. and my cousin told them that if anyone wanted to fight my little cousin, they all were going to fight him one-on-one. Now I am like awe, hell no, but heck, that's better than getting jumped and beat up. Well, what do you know? These guys did not want to fight me one-on-one. Lawd, I got a pass because they left, and I was able to go home and breathe a sigh of relief. So, I think it's over, but not so fast. School has started, and I am hanging out with my friends across town. So, I was heading home, and now I ran into the one cousin who we were good friends, and now he wanted revenge. When I saw him, he said you broke my cousin's nose, and he came after me with a knife. Now, I thought me, and this guy was good, but evidently not. I ran home so I did not get stabbed. For some reason, everyone wants to stab me. But when I got home, I was mad. Mary Gregoire asked me what happened, and I told her. And I was about to take a knife out of the house and go back after the guy. I was so mad I punched a hole in the door. Mary Gregoire did not say anything to me but let me cool off. Well, after that incident, about a week or two later, I ran into the guy again, and he came towards me. I told him I did not want to fight him. He said we were cool; my cousin was a troublemaker, and she probably deserved it. The moral of this story don't hit women.

HIGH SCHOOL

I remember my first day of school, and I was talking about high school. Look at me now; I have made it to the big leagues. One thing is for sure: everything was big in high school. I remember that as a sophomore, you had to earn the right to be considered in most groups. I remember riding on the bus, and most of the Juniors and Seniors had their personal seats. Now it's up to us sophomores to take the table scraps. I remember being on the bus and riding it with the most famous guy in the school. He was one of the biggest and an All-American in football who would go on to play in college and the NFL.

My first day of school was confusing but fun. I met up with some of the people I went to freshman high, and we had a good time. Now, I wanted to play football, and that's what I did. I went out to practice a couple of times, and then I quit football. To this day, it seems like I lost motivation because all the guys were big, and they put in the work to be on the high school team. I look back at it now. I lost the drive to go to the gym that summer, and man, did it hurt. But I quickly found my new sport, and let me tell you, I was an All-American at it. Chasing girls, yes, I loved the girls, and heck, they loved me. It was my full-time job. I am hanging out with my crew, and man, we had it going on. On Friday nights, we would go to the football games not to look at the game but to chase the girls. All I knew was girls and school, but school for me was chasing the girls. My 10th-grade year went by fast. There wasn't much to talk about other than meeting up with girls, hanging out with the guys and party after party. I am so surprised I passed the 10th grade because I barely studied and barely passed all my tests. I remember that summer coming around, and I had a summer job.

Now let me tell you this. Mary Gregoire could not afford to buy me the clothes I wanted, so I spent most of my time doing odd jobs to earn money until I turned 16 years old. Now it's game on. I wanted a job so bad that I could taste money. Nothing mattered to me, but I just got a job so I could afford to buy myself some clothes. I loved my mother, and she did all she could do to help me with school supplies and clothes. My father was the laugh of it all. I remember him taking me clothes shopping and barely breaking a 20-dollar bill for my school shopping. I remember showing my mother the clothes he brought me. One shirt, one pair of pants and one pair of shoes came out of a box that had over 100 other pairs of flash and dash tennis shoes. Lawd, we laughed, but I wore the shirt and pants because that's all I had. So, I was motivated to find a job. I remember coming home from school my sophomore year and walking my whole town once a week until I got the call from Pizza Inn. Man, I got a job, and it's game on. Now, I am making money to afford some clothes and help my mother out. Just after I got this job, Popeyes called me for a job. I am a wanted man in the job industry. It is too late, and I am a working man now. But with a job came many sacrifices.

No more football games to chase women, no hanging out with the homies; it's work and home. I'm working on school nights and back home, but heck, now I can afford the clothes. Calvin Klien and Braxton, I have all the name brands on me. You better ask somebody about Leo Gregoire. This guy looks good and is hard-working. But I remember the beginning of my 11th-grade year when I met her. The love of my life, and it was by default. She would change the course of my high school days and have a lasting impact on me for the rest of my adult life.

At the beginning of my 11th-grade year, it was business as usual. I had the job buying myself nice clothes, and there was nothing to worry about. Me and the guys I hung out with are doing our usual thing. Sitting in class cheating on the girls' papers in our classrooms. At this time, I am still working and unable to attend any of the Friday night football games, which, to me, was not important because the only thing important to me is work. Well, it just so happened that the local fair is in town, and I am off work so that I can attend the parades and the fair that night. I will never forget this day. I remember walking home from the parade and getting home. Now it's business as usual. Let me find a ride to the fair, and just so have my sister Leona going to the fair. Now, when I get to our apartment, I walk in the door, and there she is. Now, I am not going to say her name for my next book. But there she was, looking at me, and I mean looking at me. She was beautiful. But I am into my clothes and trying to get to the fair to meet up with my friends. So, I hitched a ride with my sister. Now, at the fair, I go my way doing my thing. But for some odd reason, she would bump into me to see what I was doing. From time to time, she would hang out with me. She was beautiful, and I could not take my eyes off her. Now it's time to go, and we are piled up in this car. For some reason, we have more people than we care to bargain with. Then I asked the question, how old are you. Lawd, when she told me her age, I was like, hell no, I cannot mess with you. Now peer pressure is ugly, and my sister Leona blasted me, saying boy, stop worrying about her age. You know she likes you, and you like her. There was no denying I liked her from the moment I saw her. I think my sister gave her the green light because she was smiling from head to toe. We are cramped in this car. So, my sister again tells the girl to sit on my lap so we can make space. So now she is sitting on my lap, and no lie, I am enjoying every moment, but I am still trying to be cool as usual. Now, as my memory serves me, I think we took her home first, and she looked at me and said I want a kiss, and I said OK. Dam, that was a beautiful kiss. Now, I am hooked and will be hooked my whole junior year of high school. I would see her every time she was at her grandmother's home. I had a 10-speed bike, so I would ride a dam near 10 miles to see her. Her mother was ok with us dating even though we had four years between us. But mom didn't mind, and neither did I. I was in love and man did I wear it. We went to a very important event at my school, and you could see love written all over my face. You know love will make you do crazy things. I remember I wanted to take off from work for my birthday to spend time with her. I remember putting in to be off, but my job told me no. Now, I am about to decide which will be the catalyst of many of my decisions to come. I decided to quit my job. I remember telling my mother, Mary Gregoire, that she had just looked at me. I did not care; all I wanted to do was spend time with her. I remember being invited to a New Edition concert with her and her relatives in another city. I was told the local tough guy had a crush on her. Little did I know he would show up to where we were living, and the guy wanted to fight me for her. I am so happy that did not happen because I am not a fighter just a lover, lol. Now, here is the crazy thing. During this time, I was still a virgin. In my next book, I will go into more detail as to why. I remember my first wet dream, but it was nothing. Now I remember going to visit her, and for some reason, I was there late. Later than usual. And we kissed, but this time, something strange happened. While I was kissing her, this amazing feeling started to happen. I did not know I was about to have an orgasm while kissing her. This is brand new to me. But I stopped, and I did not go all the way. But then I said the heck with it. We began kissing again, and man, did it feel good, and then it was over. I had an orgasm on myself. This would be the first of many, lol. As we continued to spend time with one another, and the school year was ending, there would be something else ending. But this close would be one of the most devastating closures of my life.

MY LIFE FOREVER CHANGED

As I begin this chapter, I would like for all the readers to know I am leaving a lot of the details out for the next book that I am writing. In no way will I speak bad or negative of any of my past relationships from the standpoint of where I am today. My life made a change the summer going into my senior year of high school. This summer, my relationship ended with her, and it devastated me. Just know this was one of the many events that led to me feeling that I was never enough. As I began my senior year of high school, I felt like I was the big dawg on campus. I was hot into the girls but not into my schoolwork. The term class clown had my name wrapped around it. It was a good life, with freedom from work because I was not working, and my mother gave me extra time for my curfew. I remember meeting the girls at the football games and not even paying attention to the games. My whole senior year was party after party. Like I said, it was the good life. I remember all I wanted to do was go to class and not do any work. In many cases, I did not do any work. I am wondering to this day why or how I graduated high school. I remember meeting up with friends before class, and we would get our drink. I remember going to class and sitting in class with shades, especially on Fridays. My life was not complicated, but I did a lot. But still, it lingered: what was she doing, and when would I see her again? I remember one Saturday night, my best friend and I were hanging out, and I do not know why. To this day, I went to her house. There at her house were guys. She evidently had her relatives in town, who were girls, and all were matched up with guys. Again, I won't go into debt with this story, but it led to an altercation between me and one of her cousins. I remember going to a school talent show where my cousin confronted me. He was larger than me. He wanted me to go to her home and apologize to her grandmother. I refused to do so. After the show was over, the guy came up to me and slapped me. In front of everyone. Little did I know this would be one of the events that led me down a road to anger and vengeance that I needed to release. I remember skipping school to find the guy. I was more afraid of him, and I didn't know what to do. You see, I never liked bullies, and he was a bully. He taunted me on many occasions. I remember him confronting me, and it was said that my best friend's cousin had spread rumors about the incident. Well, at my best friend's home, I confronted his cousin and beat him up for it. It was that day that my best friend let me beat his cousin up but warned me never to pick my hands up to him. And I love my best friend for those kind words, lol. As I got closer to the end of the school year, I remembered my grades were awful, and I was placed in a special class. Now, this class was for those people who did not want to do their work, and I will forever remember the teacher. She was a hard teacher and had a reputation for failing seniors and did not care. I was afraid of her. And when she gave the class the spill, if we did not do the work, she would fail us. I did not act like any class clown anymore. I needed an A in her class both for the exams and the semester grade. I remember every assignment I did was an A. I understood algebra, and I liked spelling my name. When it was time to get our grades, and I made an A, she told me I was very smart and too smart to be in her class. I will never forget her encouraging words. Now, it's the last day of school, and on the last day of school, it's graduation practice. But there was an issue. I still had to get my grades to find out if I had graduated. Now it's English and man, I did not like English, but the teacher was cool. I remember seeing my classmates make their way onto the field, and I was trying to get my grades. When my teacher told me my grades and that I had passed, I ran out to the field to meet them. They were looking at me, and I was happy. They laughed at me. Now I had to walk home because I missed my bus. I remember walking home, and when I came into the back door, my mother, Mary Gregoire, was right there cooking, and as usual, I got jokes. I said Mommy, I got bad news I did not graduate, and she looked at me, and then I told her I was teasing I passed. She was very happy. I kept the promise I made to her when I was in the 8th grade and that I was going to graduate high school. As I step and begin to write the next segment of this book, I would like to let the readers know that as I sit here writing this book, there are events that I have left out that will be discussed in my next book. The exciting thing about the rest of this book is that it will take everyone on my journey to the next chapters of my life.

GRADUATION

I will never forget the words Mary Gregoire said to me after the graduation party ended. In her exact words, "Son, when you are leaving," let me start the story. I remember going to my graduation, and man, it was an epic day. But let me begin by saying what the events were leading up to this day. My oldest sister came into town, and man, it was beautiful. All the graduation parties leading up to this day were epic. But something happened that would never leave my mind. I remember my aunt coming to the house saying my grandmother did not have a ride to my graduation. And man, I was sad. But the almighty big sister of mine said I will go pick her up. So, we all tightly fitted in one of the few cars we had available to us and off we went. I will never forget meeting up with my friends, and we were celebrating before we even got our diplomas. I will never forget the words of our principal when we were at a graduation party. He said not to throw your hands up, not to celebrate, and no, and he meant no jumping up and down when you get your diploma, or you will not graduate. Lawd, little did he know Leo John Gregoire Jr was going to violate that rule to no end. When everything started, I had butterflies in my stomach, and we made our way onto the field. It seemed forever. All I could think about was the graduation party. The fellas and I had rented rooms at the hotel and had our favorite drinks while sitting in the bathtub getting cold. Yep, even back then, I could have been an event planner in limbo, on to the story. We got all seated, sat through all the boring spills, and then the names got called to get our diplomas. Yes, they called all the smart people and got them out of the way. Now it's time for us, the party people. I will never forget when they got to my row; I was as hyped as they could get. I made my way on stage, and as I was sitting here, I could see the whole thing all over again. They gave me my diploma, and the principal shook my hand. Like Leo Gregoire, I looked to the crowd and raised my diploma, raising both my hands. I had a small group with me, but they were the loudest. The most heart-warming moment that will never leave my heart was when I laid eyes on my mother. Mary Gregoire's eyes locked eyes with me. And I was like a minimum of 200 meters away, but it seemed like we were 3 feet from each other. We locked eyes, and I said I did it for you in my heart. My sisters were screaming, but Mary Gregoire just smiled.

I accomplished what I said I was going to do when I was in the 8th grade. Mission accomplished. Now graduation is over, and we are celebrating on the field. The families were waiting for us. Someone tapped me and said Leo, there go your Uncle Julius. I will never forget seeing him in his work clothes. As I cried up in writing this, I remembered making my way to him and hearing him speak. Lil Leo, I am sorry I did not make it to the ceremony. I smiled and shook his hands, and with a smile on my face, I said thank you for coming. At least you are here now. You see, I was never a kid who held grudges. I always loved the simplest things. So now it's time to head home, and man, you know, party time. Well, first, celebrate with family and the celebratory toast. I had to get into my party clothes, and before hitting the streets, my Uncle Julius talked. My man, Big Lou, showed up, and we were out in the streets. I say what happened, but we partied like rock stars. Just like our Senior prom graduation night was no different. We partied.

Events in the hotel I really can't talk about that because this is a family book, but use your imagination. A young man who just graduated high school is about to go on the adventure of a lifetime. What is it called "Life?" This brings to the closing of this part of my life and the newer, and I mean the never forgetful words of the most loving mother and respected mentor I have ever had. I remember coming into the house, and Mary Gregoire said Son, you left so fast you forgot to cut your cake. I was like oh yeah, let me cut it quick. And in her loving voice and with a smile on her face, she said, Son, the parties over? I was like, yes, ma'am, the parties are over, and with the smoothest of lines, almost sounding like a jazz musician, Mary Gregoire said, son, when you are leaving.

MY DEFINING SUMMER

This summer was very different, to say the least. I knew it was my last summer being home, and I still had no plans for what I was going to do with my life. I knew one thing for certain: I was going to find a job because Mary Gregoire wanted me out of the house, and she could not afford to give me money. I had a childhood friend who was moving to Colorado and offered me the opportunity to come out there and find a job. So, I decided that at the end of summer, this is where I am headed. One thing is for sure: Mary Gregoire was hard, but she was fair. My summer was good for me, and the fellas had a lot of fun. We did the stuff knowing we were now entering the workforce as grownups. We still danced in the streets, chased females and lived like we had no responsibilities. Oh, how that changed. By this time, I had a summer job working with the summer program called Manpower. This was a place where kids coming from families who did not make a lot of money had the opportunity to get a job to assist the family. So, I am working at a vocational school as a handyman with a crew of guys from my side of town. Man, it felt like hard work, knowing it was only for the summer. But I needed this job so I could afford to hang out and party. Now, during this time, the armed forces were knocking at my door. Man, I did not want to join the military. I remember this one guy I went to school with was trying to recruit me, and every time he called my house, I would hang up in his face. To this day, I am so sorry I did that. He and I are good friends. But all of them were at me like I was a star recruit. During this time, I also cut grass for my grandmother and aunties. I started getting closer to my grandmother and strengthening our relationship. Little did I know that it would be my last summer to see her again. My grandmother was getting sick, and soon, she would leave me in the physical and join my spirit team. So, as the summer was ending, I had an event that would change the trajectory of my plans. I will never forget this day. I remember me and the fellas were painting this room at work. And like young adults, we joke and clown around, and we get the job done. I did not realize we spilled some paint on the floor, but it was a little. When we finish the job, we will clean it up. Now comes in the boss man. He saw the paint on the floor and got mad. He was heated hotter than fish grease. He made a comment that would stick in my mind, and that was the trigger. He fussed at us while we were painting and said we painted like a bunch of monkeys. Now, he commented while we were still painting, but for some odd reason, no one heard his comment except me. I am asking myself if anyone else has just heard what I have just heard. I mean, no one has heard him say this. They all kept painting. I am like, what in the hell is going on here? Now, Bossman was Caucasian, but he was not racist. So, after hearing this, I had a decision to make. Either I stay here, or I leave and join the military. Now, let me back up. I met with a recruiter, and I am not going to say his name, but I met with him. So, I told him no, also. Now, back to the present. So now I am at a crossroads. Stay in this building or join the army. Now, Mary Gregoire did not want me to join the Army or have anything to do with the military. But it was my life; Mary Gregoire wanted me out of the house, so it's on. I am joining the Army. I left that job on the spot. No one saw me leave. I jogged 4 miles to my house, called the recruiter, and asked how soon I could leave. He was happier than a kid in a candy store that I wanted to join. Now, here comes the part where I must tell Mary Gregoire what I have decided to do. When she came home from work, I broke the news to her. I said Mommy, I joined the Army. She just gave me this look. I can still see it, but my reason was profound. I told her I was joining the Army because if I stayed there, I would get into trouble. Mary Gregoire said son, I don't want you to join the military, but it's your decision. That was one of the happiest days of my life and one of the best decisions of my life. I will never forget the day I had to leave to go to the MEPS station to do my physical and get sworn in. Let me tell you, I was scared and excited at the same time. Here it is, a small-town country boy from New Iberia, Louisiana, who was about to join the Army. We are all at the Greyhound bus station waiting for the bus to come. We are all happy. All my sisters, minus my oldest, she were in Texas, but we spoke on the phone. Now, here is the crazy part: the whole scene went from a celebration and a dam funeral to a dam quick when that Greyhound bus pulled up. All my sisters and, hell, Mary Gregoire started crying. I have never seen Mary Gregoire cry, but she did. And all I could think about was, heck, you wanted me out of the house.

GIVING THANKS

I give thanks to the Universe, God, and Source Energy for giving me the blessings of writing my first book of many. I am so thankful to have started sharing my experiences with the world, knowing that the individuals who pick up my books and read them will have the strength and power to change their lives. My books are written to inspire change in the collective consciousness. We are divine beings, and we have all the gifts of the Infinite. Thank you for reading this book, and please ensure you read my next book, which will continue the journey into Leo's life. Thank you.